Red Flags: What Single Women Should Know

Red Flags

What Single Women Should Know

30 Days of Exhortation

Penny Suber Staten

Carmen Beach Publishing Company

Publishing by Carmen Beach Publishing Co.

Copyright 2021 by Penny Suber Staten
All rights reserved.

Red Flags
What Single Women Should Know
30 Days of Exhortation

ISBN: 978-09914306-1-1

Please send your comments to the address below:
Thank you in advance.

Staten Ministries
P.O. Box 35
Tomball, Texas 77377
Email: Statenministries@gmail.com
Phone: 713.589.5779

Printed in the United States of America.

Dedication

To the young woman in whom God has poured so much beauty, so much joy, so much laughter, though these things drift from time to time.

To the grown woman who laid herself open to love and to be loved.

To the lady who gives her all to everyone who is anyone to her and even those who have become nothing at all to her.

I am writing so that she will know that she is not forgotten by God. I am writing that she will know that He hears her prayers and captures the tears she cries when she is lying alone at night in her bed, wishing to be held by her husband, even though she is not married *yet*.

I am writing to encourage her to live righteously. I am writing to encourage her to serve God with her gifts and talents, and they are many. I am writing to tell her again that God has a plan for her *right now*, in her singleness, though she may have heard it just yesterday. I am writing in hopes that she, too, will work while she is waiting.

I am writing to tell her that what she longs for in a man, she has in God. I am writing in hopes that she will trust Him as He moves in situations and in circumstances around her. I am writing to inform her that though she cannot see Him, He sees her. I am writing to tell her that He is her provider, her protector, her High Priest, her confidant, her best friend and the lover of her soul. I am hoping that she will come to know that no man will ever love her the way He does, the way He has, the way He will.

I am writing to the young lady, the grown woman to let her know that in His Word there is safety and protection from situations and circumstances that we are led to and fight through when chasing the need to be loved or the desire to be *in* love.

I am writing this exhortation so that she will take time with God, draw closer to Him; consider His Word, find strength and take comfort in them. I am sending red flags to the unmarried woman so that she will avoid some of the pit falls I fell into and confidently walk along this path God has set before her, on her way to the next destination in her life.

Introduction

But exhort one another every day, as long as it is called
"today," that none of you may be hardened by the
deceitfulness of sin.
—Hebrews 3:13 ESV

I am only one voice but a part of a multitude of counsellors. I am a part of a circle of women who pray for you, who want the best for you, who sometimes come on a little too strong but only out of love and concern for you. I am a voice of many of your sisters who would that you take heed to the wisdom that comes from experience – the experience of waiting, wondering, and wandering.

This exhortation is perhaps unconventional, but it captures a few things I want to tell the single woman who is eagerly anticipating her mate and I need more than a few words to tell it right. Perhaps you have heard these things before, but I want to put my two cents in, if you will allow me. If your single season is anything like mine was, it is a challenge, to say the least. There are good days and bad. There are declarations and there are questions. There are fresh beginnings and sorrowful endings, but all with a lesson to be grabbed and held on to.

The truth of the matter is some ways that we think and some things that we do need to be stopped. All along our journey there are warning flags that we fail to see. More often than not we are driven by what we feel and sometimes what we feel dictates what we see. This can lead us down a pathway of pain and disappointment. I don't want that for you.

In my own season, I found truths about God that I did not know. I found treasures within myself that I had not discovered. I found thumbprints in my relationships with others that I did not see. These truths steadied my Christ-like walk and calmed my human-like fears as I waited for God to move in my life. And then, He did.

For the next 30 days I want to share some of them with you. Just give me about 5-7 minutes per day. Can you do that? I have wise counsel for you. I pray that you will consider this counsel while on *your* journey with God as He prepares you for something greater in Him.

Some Things To Know About God!

Day 1: He Is Righteously, Right There

If you have ever wondered if He is there, if He is listening, if He sees you or if He even cares, I want you to know that He is with you.

God is our refuge and strength, a very present
help in trouble.
–Psalm 46:1 KJV

Sometimes it's hard to see others on the move when you're stagnant. Family, friends and foe all move in and out of relationships as if they were moving on a basketball court. Though they may not be meaningful relationships, they *are* relationships. These ladies in your circle are at least in the game. Some are able to pick and choose who they will spend time with. Some find pleasure and sometimes pain in spending their life with that special someone. But there you are, sitting on the sideline, watching and waiting. Because you want *something* special with *someone* special, "the game" is not necessarily for you; but how long must you sit there – watching, waiting and wondering. I have uttered these words myself "God, where are you?" Many times, I have cried these words "Don't you see me?"

My sister, Scripture is more than adequate in answering questions like these. Not only does it tell us where our Father is, but it tells us who He is, what He does and how we are to respond to Him. If you've only read a few stories or a few chapters, even better a few books in the Bible, you will find His character to be consistent all of the way through. His station does not change. He is *righteously right there*.

Righteously –God is the Creator and the Ruler of the universe. He has made all things and controls them accordingly. He is sovereign. Psalm 115:3 says, "But our God is in the heavens; He does whatever He pleases." He has the right because of Genesis 1:1. When you create art, music, delicacies, poetry or projects, don't you have the right to rule over that which you have created? Don't you have the power to say how the creation will move, when it will move, if it moves at all? Yes, and so it is with God. He has the authority to determine the events in your life.

Right– Christians take comfort in the truth of God's love, His mercy, His grace, but we must not forget His holiness. He is light and in Him there is no darkness (1 John 1:5). Our God is pure and good. He *is* the moral standard. He makes no mistakes – in what He does, how He does it or when He does it. He is right; moreover, He requires that we live right. 1 Peter 1:15 says "but like the Holy One who called you, be holy yourselves also in all your behavior; because it is written "YOU SHALL BE HOLY, FOR I AM HOLY." Your effort to live righteously is pivotal in all seasons of your life.

There – Finally, be assured that God is present. He has not left His creation to manage itself, as some believe. He is intimately and providentially involved with everything and everyone He has created. This can be conflicting to read because we do not always feel His presence, His intimacy with us. Could it be we are not intimate with Him? We may not always see Him because often times we overlook Him. We may not hear Him because of the noise that appeases our souls, blocking out the quiet whisper of God. Yet He is present – very present, a very present help.

Red Flag: God is not far away, unconcerned about your desires and your needs. Don't allow for doubt. Doubts have no truth in them. They will only be stumbling blocks in your life's journey. I pray that starting today you will know that He sees exactly where you are and knows exactly where you want to be.

Day 2: You Can Believe Him

If you have ever asked yourself if you can believe what He says, who He says He is and if He's going to do what He says He will, the answer is: You can.

God is not a man, that he should lie, or a son of man, that he should change his mind. Has he said, and will he not do it? Or has he spoken, and will he not fulfill it?
–Numbers 23:19 ESV

What an oxymoron – believers being called "believers" when belief is what we struggle with the most. It seems we only choose to believe what we have already seen. Our minds have decided that which entered our eye gate is true and real. We choose to believe that which was told to us in our youth; our hearts being opened to the one who nurtured and kept us from harm.

Think about this– when you were a child, it was your family, your inner circle that was the source of truth. Whatever your mom or dad said, your grandparents, your kindergarten teacher said, you believed it. You were like a sponge, soaking up everything you saw and everything you heard.

But as time went on, you began to experience life independent of your family's shadow. You learned what disappointment felt like. Misrepresentations *or lies* introduced themselves into your young, innocent world and you quickly discovered that what you see is not always what you get. Before you knew it, you have believed so many things that were not true; even some things you witnessed with your own eyes (and your own hearts) you found were not true. *Everything that glitters is not gold.*

Maybe there were things that you asked God for and you read that if you ask anything in prayer and believe it, you will receive it (Matthew 21:22). However, He did not oblige you and you still don't know why. Or perhaps you feel as if you have been delighting in the LORD for a while; yet you are still waiting for the desires of your heart to be given to you (Psalm 37:4). At this point, you may be struggling with whether or not you believe Him; but you don't want to be irreverent and say that you do not.

I, too, found myself in a crisis of belief. It was tearing and dividing my soul. I had been working in ministry but there I was—not sure of what I believed, simply because I did not understand what God was doing in my life. There were many times that I wanted to walk away from my beliefs, but I had to say to God like Simon Peter said to Jesus "Lord, to whom shall I go? You have the words of eternal life, and I have believed and have come to know that you are the Holy One of God" (John 6:68). Who else is the Giver of life? Who else could sustain me?

It was at that point, that I *decided* to believe God and it gave me mobility. Belief gives me the ability to stand on God's Word, to roll with it and to walk through whatever challenges are placed in my path. I made a conscious decision that no matter what my life looks like, no matter how I feel – alone or lonely, forgotten about, betrayed or otherwise, I will still believe. I decided to go back to believing the One who nurtures me, who keeps me from harm, the One who keeps me at peace when life seems to be falling apart. He is the One who looks out for me.

Red Flag: You can believe God and everything that He says. I pray that you will choose to believe Him today. You will have nothing to stand on if you do not.

Day 3: Committing Your Ways to Him is Essential to Your Journey With Him

Have you ever asked yourself "Why is it that I am incapable of committing to anything?" I want you to know that you are not incapable; you've just been working from your own power.

Commit your way to the LORD, trust also in Him,
and He will do it.
—Psalm 37:5 NASB 2020

In the Christian community many of us are quick to acknowledge how much we love the LORD and are emotionally moved when we reminisce on the things He has done for us – the miracles, the deliverances, the healings. Yet these same emotions can move us far away from Him when we can't see Him and are not sure if He sees us.

It is so easy to devote our time, our talents and our treasures to God when we can track Him, when we can trace Him. But once the view becomes obscure, once the sweet aroma of Him seemingly fades (because He has not moved upon request) our commitment begins to fade, losing its luster.

For many of us, if the truth were told, it's not just our commitment to Him that we struggle with. We struggle with commitments to relationships, projects, diets or other life changing, positive behaviors. I asked around and this is the feedback I got (some verbatim and others summarized):

"Too many past failures, I don't even want to try again."

"I don't want to do what someone else tells me to do, I want to do my own thing."

"If I commit to something then I'll have to be accountable to the other people involved."

I agree with all three but when it comes to the commitment Christ made to us (...in that while we were still sinners, Christ died for us – Romans 5:8) do we not owe him the commitment no matter how we feel? John 13:1 says he loved us and loved us to the end. He never faltered. He stayed the course, gave up everything in heaven and then on earth, to keep the commitment.

Should we not wake up every morning with the same purpose no matter what is going on in our lives, in our minds or in our hearts? David, in his maturity, wrote Psalm 37 to instruct us on how to handle our feelings about those around us who do evil and seem to prosper in spite of that fact. We often get sidetracked when we do not see our own goals being fulfilled in the face of the success of others, especially of those who are not committed to God themselves. He basically says "Listen, don't focus on that mess. Focus on you and your walk with the LORD. "Commit your way...."

In this text, commit means to roll. God wants us to roll our ways into Him. What are our ways? It's our habitual manners, our modes, our methods, our plans, our means for attaining goals. God wants those things to be rolled in or with Him, but we cannot do this in our own might. It is the Holy Spirit that empowers us to stay committed to God. The Holy Spirit helps us in our weakness (Romans 8:26). If we want to be more committed to God but we do not have it within ourselves to change, know that He is the change agent.

Look at Psalm 37:4. The Scripture declares that if we delight ourselves in the Lord, He will give us the desires of our hearts. It then goes on to the Scripture for today. It calls for us to commit our ways to Him. Committing our way means that we will first consider His instructions before we do what we do, remembering that He is the plumbline for our righteous living, our moral compass. Commit your way to the LORD, Trust in Him and He will bring *it* to pass. What is the *it*? It appears to be that which you are desiring.

What if I asked you about your commitment to the Lord? What would your answer be?

Red Flag: Your journey with Christ requires an intentional commitment that must be renewed every day. If you cannot commit to Him, how will you ever commit to someone else? My prayer is that you will use the power of the Holy Spirit to help you with your commitments to the things of God today.

Day 4: What You Really Need to Know is This

If there has ever been a thought in your mind that where you will spend eternity, that depends on you.

For "everyone who calls on the name of the Lord
will be saved."
–Romans 10:13 ESV

This exhortation is written as a red flag to the single woman in hopes that she will take a few days and consider her journey with God, her day-to-day practices and her relationships with others before she walks down a dangerous path. All of these are important on her journey as a single woman but if she does not have Christ, none of these things matter.

The only thing that truly matters is the destination at the end of the journey, eternal life. There are many views about eternity. The one I speak of is the truth about our souls continuing on after this life on earth has passed. Know for sure that your life will continue. Where it will continue is the question that I cannot answer, but you can.

If you've never made a decision about eternity, it is imperative that you do so today. I encourage you to complete this exhortation, but some ideas may be foreign if you are not a Christian. Let me take time to share a few Scriptures found in Romans that may simplify what we believe.

Romans 3:23 For all have sinned and fall short of the glory of God.

Romans 6:23 For the wages of sin is death, but the gift of God is eternal life in Christ Jesus our Lord.

Romans 5:8 But God demonstrates His own love toward us, in that while we were still sinners, Christ died for us.

Romans 10:9, 10:13…that if you confess with your mouth the Lord Jesus and believe in your heart that God has raised Him from the dead, you will be saved. For with the heart one believes unto righteousness, and with the mouth confession is made unto salvation…(13) for whoever calls on the name of the Lord will be saved.

Red Flag: A life without Jesus Christ is death. Salvation through Jesus Christ is available to you. His is the only name by which man can be saved. Nothing in this life will ever come close to our eternal reward in Christ. I pray that if you have not confessed Christ as your Savior, you will do so today.

Day 5: God Already Knows it All

*If you've ever doubted that God sees you and knows you —
every part of you, you need to know about Psalm 139.*

You have looked deep into my heart, LORD,
and you know all about me.
—Psalm 139:1 CEV

One of my unmarried lady friends worked in the office that I worked in. We were 6 feet apart for "social distancing", totally alone in the department for an hour every day before others arrived. Every morning we had our private chat, and I would ask how she slept, just for conversation's sake. Some mornings the answer was "I slept well," other mornings the answer was contrary to that. I offered one of two answers:

"Oh no, I hate that." *Or*

"Why is that? What's on your mind?"

To the former she would respond "I know, right."

To the latter, she would respond, "Oh nothing, just couldn't sleep."

I wondered if she would ever get to the point of telling me the truth. After all, we had been shut away from the world of others, confined to this smaller area for about year, at that point. We shared so many intimate thoughts and looked out for each other during the challenge that was 2020. But she never felt comfortable enough to share her emotional pain with me, her doubts, her fears of being single for the rest of her life. What if, after she had given all of herself to her daughters, who were on the brink of adulthood, she would have nothing to live for and no-one to share life with? I was familiar with the questions, familiar with the look, familiar with the morning silence after a sleepless night of wondering because it was once me.

Better than that, God was familiar. He knows all the thoughts, the questions and the fears. Although she could not share her deepest thoughts with me (these may have even been too deep for her), she could openly and honestly share them with God. There's a Scripture that says you can ask God for wisdom and He will freely give it *without reproach**(James 1:5). He says He won't judge us. He won't make us feel bad about what we've done or haven't done, what we know or don't know. I think He wants us to confess our weaknesses, our hurts, our failures, even our failures to understand what's going on in our lives. He won't make us feel bad about it.

Psalm 139 is one of my favorites. We suffer with this idea that no one understands us or knows the depths of our thoughts. Many times, *we* do not understand our thoughts or are unable to articulate them. But David's psalm tells us that God knows us and understands our thoughts even before we are able to speak them. He created our innermost parts. The Scripture says "How precious also are your thoughts for me, God! How vast is the sum of them!" Then, he invites God to search him, to know his heart and anxious thoughts, and put him to the test. We should too, as we wrestle with these questions in the wee hours of the morning. God already knows us and what is in our hearts. He wants to have a conversation with us about what's there. He invites us to cast our cares upon Him (Psalm 55:22).

Red Flag: It's important that your line of communication is open with God. Make sure it is not tainted. Tell Him what's on your mind and then Go. To. Sleep. Tonight.

*emphasis added.

Day 6: You Don't Need a Prescription for Anxiety, God is Your Healer

If you've ever asked yourself why your emotions are all over the place or why restful nights are few and far between, you need to know that the peace of God can sometimes escape you.

Do not be anxious about anything, but in every situation, by prayer and petition, with thanksgiving, present your requests to God. And the peace of God, which transcends all understanding, will guard your hearts and your minds in Christ Jesus.

—Philippians 4:6-7 NIV

Did you know that you can be in perfect health, be as beautiful as a runway model and your soul can be in so much turmoil that you cannot sleep at night? When in those quiet moments, you become uncomfortable? Turn on the television? Call someone, anyone, to talk to? Does your mind ever turn off or is it always wondering about the future, always questioning the events of the past, trying to make sense of them?

Life can be fast—full of rapidly moving activity that ultimately means nothing. It can be noisy—full of sounds that make no sense or worse, sounds that make sense but is of no real value, no truth in the end. The only peace you will find is in the quiet, still moments that you invite the Holy Spirit to.

Life can be fast. You make decisions according to what you feel in the moment and then the feeling changes; then you are left with the consequences of the swift moving emotion that caught you off guard.

Life can be noisy. Between this advice show, that life coach, the FaceBook post and the woman you follow on TikTok, you are inundated with information on how to, why to and when to whatever it is you're thinking about doing *right now*.

You see so much. You hear and feel so much yet these things don't connect to each other. It only plants seeds of doubt and truth becomes more obscured. You find yourself asking, like Pontus Pilot asked Jesus, "What is truth?" It's important that you stop the madness in your life and seek truth – about yourself.

At the end of the day, you may use outside noise to keep the inside noise at bay. Your head hits the pillow and the energy spent on work and the kids and school and the church and Momma and BFF is zapped from you, but then 2 am comes or maybe it's 3 am. Eyes wide open. What are you thinking about? What is your heart desiring from God and why don't you have it yet? Is He keeping it from you? Or are you keeping it from yourself? Is it financial security? Is it a better job? Is it physical healing? Or emotional healing? Is it a husband? Or just someone to talk to? Is it wholeness in your family? Are you coveting what your sister in the Lord has? Are you jealous of her? Is it forgiveness – you want to forgive someone and cannot? Or you want forgiveness from God, and you do not realize that you already have it? Is it Him? Or is it you?

Can I submit to you that we will find fault within ourselves before we can ever find the slightest bit of fault in God? There are no nuances in God. The New Testament writers say there is no variation in Him, no shifting shadow (James 1:17); there is no darkness in Him at all (1 John 1:5). Many times we do not understand why He does what He does, but our trust in Him takes up the gap of our understanding. Therefore, we must turn inward to check if *our* hearts are aligned with the word of God, and if our words and actions attest to it. This is not on the surface, my sister, but a deep searching of the soul.

In many cases, we do the best we can to live according to Scripture. We are compelled to turn back to God and ask about the promise He made to us and its fulfillment. Our fathers in the faith had to wait – Abraham for Isaac, David for the throne. Even when we search deeply within ourselves and an answer is returned to us, we must be at peace with the wait and at peace with the will of God for our lives, including the wait. Meanwhile we must work in the busyness and rest in the quietness, knowing that our hearts are clear with God and trusting in His timing.

Red Flag: Be anxious for NO THING starting this day. Know that when you are aligned with the word of God, you have nothing to be anxious for. Earthly remedies are just that – earthly, temporary, partial. I pray that you will seek God if your soul is in need of healing this day.

Day 7: You Must be Real With God and With Yourself

I want you to know that you can be real with God about wherever you are in your walk with Him.

"…Yet in spite of all this her treacherous sister Judah did not return to Me with all her heart, but rather in deception," declares the LORD. And the LORD said to me, "Faithless Israel has proved herself to be more righteous than treacherous Judah…"
—**Jeremiah 3:10-11 NASB 2020**

Trying to impress someone is hard work. While you're still trying to decide if he is "the one" you may find yourself "going along to get along." You may change what you wear or what you eat; "Eat healthier" they say. You may go new places. You may sit through a horror movie, scared out of your mind! Or to a museum, bored out of your mind! "Broaden your horizons" they say and because you're going along to get along, you pretend to agree and be something you are not – at least while you're in his car. But are your being real with him? Are you being real with yourself?

In the case of God, what He desires for you is not simply based on His opinion, His style or His preference; but what God desires for you is the very best based on His love for you, His plan for your life and His omniscience through all eternity. The question is do you truly want what God desires for you, or do we want what you want? You see, even with God, we can find ourselves "going along to get along."

Single women are encouraged that there is one who God has purposed for their lives and usually respond favorably at its hearing. They hope for and look for the one God has set aside for their good; but as days go by and that "one" does not surface, they lull back into trying to work with whoever is present and answers the roll call in their lives. I'm speaking from personal experience. Perhaps he is not the one God has "purposed" or "set aside" for you (if you subscribe to this thought process), but he is present and accounted for. Forget the incompatibility, the disconnect, and the other red flags that say "Go the other way!" A steady and committed relationship is what you want.

It's not just with relationships. Many Christians, in general, want what we want in other areas of our lives. We dictate our career paths, where we live, our role in our community, in our church, etc., perhaps all without considering how we may best please God – what it is that He wants from us and for us. Is this important to you?

Wanting what God wants may be important to some and not very important to others. Be honest with yourself and by all means keep it real. When you pray (for whatever) are you considering what God wants for you? I know you're asking for what you want and that's surely permissible. In fact, He wants us to ask, and He certainly wants to bless us. But we dare not submit our list of "Father, can you do this" and "Please God, will you do that" without first yielding it to His will.

Yielding our will to God's will is not easily arrived at. We know what we want out of our lives. We have a picture of our future and we may even know what it takes to get there, especially those of us who are creative, educated, motivated and foolish enough to believe we hold the key to our own destiny and only consider ourselves when making decisions. We're just keeping it real, right?

At some point, we've got to ask ourselves do we want what we want for us, in our finite knowledge and ability, or do we want what God wants for us. Though it may not always feel good, taste good or look good going through the process, do we desire His outcome for our lives or are we trusting our own plan? Are we "going along to get along" *with God*?

I submit that it is critical that we are honest about where we are. If we are not there yet, then we are not there yet. We still want what we want. Keep it real. But here's something you can do that is just as real. You can go to the Father and request an earnest desire to want what He wants for you. In one season of my journey with God, I was living as if I had already given my will over to God's will and it may have looked like I wanted what He wanted but I did not. Here's what I'm talking about.

Years ago, I went through a divorce. I may have thought I was yielding my will to God's will because I finally gave up on the marriage. I discontinued the fight against my husband's quest to leave after fighting for years to keep our family together. I had read in the Bible how God felt about divorce, and I wanted to avoid it believing that is what I wanted. But His releasing me from that marriage (see 1 Corinthians 7:15) was actually a relief to me. My marriage was like living with an angry lion who just wanted to be free no matter what. Hindsight, I was actually lying to myself every time I persuaded him to return home to a life he did not want with a wife who could not fail. Shortly afterwards something that I wanted all of my life was in the palm of my hand. Then it slipped through my fingers. I thought I wanted what God wanted for me but when I suffered this loss, I realized I just wanted what I wanted. I would pray to regain it – at whatever cost, regardless of the situation. Then it came to me that perhaps it was not what God wanted for me. This hurt me deeply because of my affections; but in my brokenness, I came to love God more and embraced the truth that He knows what is best for me and that is what He desires for me.

I don't wish that type of pain upon anyone. But it uncovered my true desire to please myself above all else; so, for me, it was worth it. My sister, you have a chance now, hopefully without being in a stressful or painful situation, to evaluate where you are. Do you want what you want, or do you want what God wants for you? Be real with yourself.

Red Flag: Don't fool yourself. Search the motives of your desires. Use my story to try to identify them. If they are selfish, I pray that today you will ask God to replace them with a desire to please Him by yielding your desires to His.

Day 8: Your Obedience to Him Keeps Unnecessary Pain Out

I want you to know that obedience is not for God; it is for us.

But Samuel replied: "Does the LORD delight in burnt offerings
and sacrifices as much as in obeying the LORD? To obey is
better than sacrifice, and to heed is better
than the fat of rams…"
—I Samuel 15: 22 NIV

Parenthood gave me a different perspective, deeper appreciation and love for God the Father, than I can say. The all-time best selling how-to book on parenting is the Bible. The most valuable counsel that money *can not* buy is found in the example of our Heavenly Father. In His parenting, we find sacrifice, love, devotion, commitment, long-suffering, patience, kindness, discipline, understanding, wisdom, comfort, provision, creativity and the list goes on.

God the Father has a perfect plan for each of His children. But many times, we neglect the role we play in His plan for us – our obedience. He has given us a wonderful gift called "free-will". It is indeed a gift in that we are allowed to exercise our decision making, our creativity and the *management* of our lives. Free will allows us to express our likes and our dislikes. Our uniqueness complements our free will. On the other hand, this gift, if mishandled, can be a detriment.

Somehow, because we are allowed to make our own choices in life, we live under the impression that our life is our own. If you're a believer, the Scripture says otherwise (I Corinthians 6:19-20). If you're not a believer, the Scripture says otherwise

(Psalm 24:1). I mentioned a moment ago the "management" of our lives, not the "ownership" of our lives. We say things like "I control my destiny," "I'm not accountable to anyone," or my favorite, "I'm a grown woman."

What we've done with our "grown selves" is created a lifestyle of making decisions based on our limited knowledge, our incomplete understanding, our unstable hearts and our misinterpreted experiences. And where did those decisions lead us? Perhaps sometimes to a good place but more often than not, if we've made a decision without consulting the Wonderful Counselor, we either made several complete circles or ended up in a straight line headed in the wrong direction with a lot of unnecessary pain.

Even though we don't like the outcome of some of our decisions, something about obeying God's word doesn't set right with us either. Could it be because we were born in direct opposition to it – hostile towards God (Colossians 1:21)? When we think of the word *obedience*, does a picture of a fence enter our minds? A fence that corrals us to a certain way of doing things which leads to a uniformed, under stimulated, uneventful lifestyle? No fun, right? Does God not want us to enjoy our lives?

On the contrary, He wants us to experience the fullness of life. You will come to find, as I have, that the temporary pleasures of life that are done in disobedience to God are just that – temporary pleasures. When they feel good, they feel really good – the act of disobedience. When they feel bad, they feel really bad, and they *are* really bad. As a matter of fact, the bad feelings far outweigh the good feelings, not to mention the consequences that follow disobedience.

Understand, my sister, that when you are obeying our Father, it is not for *His* benefit. It is for yours. He is not in danger of losing anything because everything belongs to Him. There are no consequences for God. There is no judgement of His character, His actions. But on the contrary for His creation, there are consequences and ultimately there is judgement – for the decisions we make in this life.

Red Flag: Remember that obedience is for your benefit. The fence is not there to keep you inside, but it is there to keep the enemy outside. On this day ask the Lord to give you a desire to read His word so that you will know when you are too close to the fence and certainly when you have stepped outside of it.

Day 9: There are no Knock Outs Just Knock Downs—You Need to Know the Difference

Don't get it twisted. Believers are not knocked out, never to return; we're only knocked down, only get back up.

If we confess our sins, he is faithful and just and will forgive us our sins and purify us from all unrighteousness.
—I John 1:9 NIV

The practice of righteous living is not achieved overnight. It will take time. It will take planning. It will take submission. There will be good times and bad times; loneliness and togetherness; tearing down and building up; triumph and defeat. Some evenings you may be on top of the world because you have just experienced the greatest day of our life! You found intimacy on a whole different level and you were completely satisfied. Most importantly, you ended the day with the same integrity you started it with. How cool is that?

But then there may be some nights when the lighting is just right, the music is soft and your accountability partner is somewhere in the country at a family reunion with no cell phone towers and boy howdy! It's on! The next morning you're leaning on the side of the bed, feeling like the scum underneath your oldest shoe; like you have lied to yourself thinking you could abstain; like you are no better than any lady of the night; like you have not only let yourself down, but you have let God down.

But that's not the only sin that can knock us down. There are plenty of others. Been there; done that – knocked down. This is not where God wants you to be so don't stay down; get up.

While you're down there, get on your knees and earnestly repent your sins - yielding to the temptation and committing the act – then get up and be assured of God's forgiveness.

Now let's be clear, to repent is to change your mind; agree with God concerning sin. Repenting does not mean you continue in the sin after you apologize. It is not your apologize that God requires. It is your repentance, your agreement with God and your earnest effort to stop it.

Read Romans 7:14-25. The Apostle Paul talks about the ongoing struggle of the natural man and the spirit man, the man who is born once and the man who is born again respectively. Paul made himself transparent and relative. There's a continuous war going on between our minds and our bodies. As we continue to live this life, some battles we will win and some we will lose but we are assured the war is won. *There is now no condemnation for those of us who are in Christ Jesus* (Romans 8:1 NIV).

God does not stand over us and count backwards from ten challenging us to rise by our own strength. No. It is only the enemy who kneels down as we lay paralyzed on the ground and whispers in our ear that it is over when we fail to overcome our sinful nature. He does not want us to know that we have all we need to stand up again.

The Scripture says "His divine power has given us everything we need for life and godliness *through the knowledge of him who called us** by his own glory and excellence" (2 Peter 1:3 ESV). We lack nothing to overcome our sinful nature.

But when we fall, no matter how many times, God is waiting there to wipe away sins, to heal and forgive, to offer another chance to get it right. The Holy Spirit gives us new wind, new

*emphasis added

energy and a new drive to get back in the fight. My sister, do not give up on your pursuit of righteous living. Do not allow disappointment or shame to keep you from trying again.

Red Flag: Be confident in your righteous walk starting this day. You must know that God has equipped you with everything you need to resist temptation, be confident in doing so, and be confident in forgiveness when you don't. Without this confidence, you will always beat yourself up and you may never know the forgiving graces of God.

Some Things to Know About Yourself if You are Going to Live Righteously!

Day 10: You Must Have a Daily Devotion

If you need to know why you can't seem to find the time to read the Bible, it's because you don't know how important it is and the enemy knows just how important it is.

I have treasured Your word in my heart, so that I may not sin against You.
—Psalm 119: 11 NASB 2020

One of the worse mistakes Christians make is underestimating the word of God. Life can be likened to a complicated piece of machinery (let's say…an Apple). It's got many moving parts, it does things on its own without you even knowing. It has functions that you will probably never use and that functionality can only be executed by you, either by password or by face recognition. What you do in one area automatically shows up in another. If you break it, you have to wait for a specialist in order to fix it. It comes with the ability to connect to others. It's connected to something higher and wider that knows you before you know it. It updates while you're sleeping and every couple of years there's something new about it, so you'll have to trade it in to keep up with the times.

Whether you own an IPad, IPhone or one of those things that look like a watch but it's really not, the first time you used it, you probably read something about it (unlike a man). Though you may have been familiar with the product (you may have seen others use it – sometimes successfully, sometimes not) this one was *yours*. It was expensive, delicate and only you were responsible for keeping it in the best shape you possibly could.

My sister, our lives are like that – expensive, delicate and only we (as individuals) are responsible for keeping it in the best shape we possibly can. Just like the Apple product and anything of value, instructions come with the package. It tells us how to use it, how to get the best use of it and how to prolong its use. For our lives, the most valuable commodity placed in our care, the Bible is the manual and it is multi-purposeful.

The God-breathed Scripture is God's unmatched wisdom written for us to use for daily living. Every single day presents the question "How should I live?" What you will hear in your mind is "What do I do about this or that?" Every. Single. Day. Freedom to choose how we will live is exciting and inviting until we find that we do not have the answers leading us to the best outcome for our lives. We only see what is right in front of us. We rarely have a complete understanding of it; and to add insult to injury, we can't even be sure of what we will run into next. But the word of God is our navigator.

The Bible is often called a "love-letter" because in it we will find the words of God written to us so that we will know Him, His character and how much He loves us. In it we find Him glorious, spectacular, awesome in might and power. We find that He is consistent, trustworthy and dutiful. When we read the history of God's people, including our own history as Christians, we see how He has redeemed us, restored us, kept us and continues to look out for us.

God's word is a liniment. It comforts and heals when life hurts. Life hurts when we do not follow the instructions of God; and sometimes even when we do. It also convicts us when we have done wrong and when we haven't (but we thought about it). The Bible helps us to watch; it helps us to wait, and it helps us to work in the meantime. It is multi-purpose. I could probably use other metaphors and describe it in more ways, but the Apostle Paul said it better than I ever could in his letter to Timothy.

All Scripture is God-breathed and is useful for teaching, rebuking, correcting and training in righteousness. (2 Timothy 3:16 NIV)

Red Flag: God's word is essential to your life. There is never a time in your spiritual life that you should not be studying the Bible *(not just a religious publication or a devotional but the Bible).*

Day 11: You Need Some Suggestions on Where to Start! I Got You

Want good success?

This Book of the Law shall not depart from your mouth, but you shall meditate on it day and night, so that you may be careful to do according to all that is written it in. For then you will make your way prosperous, and then you will have good success.
—Joshua 1:8 ESV

1. **Start with realistic goals.** There is no need to try to impress God. He made you and He knows you better than you know yourself. There is no shame in starting with 15 to 30 minutes of your day, if that's what you can realistically set aside. The goal is to spend time with God in consecrated devotion *every day*. So, whether it is 15 minutes, 50 minutes, or 5 hours, carve out uninterrupted time for you and God – reading and praying. Time *set aside* allows you to talk with Him and allots time to settle your spirit so that He can talk to you. This time is so special that it will seamlessly increase over time.

2. **Start with the Gospels.** My preference is John, then Mark; Matthew then Luke. Each book records the life and works of our Savior, Jesus Christ. Each writer tells the story but for a different reason and sometimes from a different vantage point. Before you start reading a book in the Bible, read a brief commentary on it. It will help you focus in on what God is saying to you.

3. **Follow up according to your own taste in literature.**

   o   Acts of the Apostles, the history of the church. It follows the Gospel of Luke and will continue the story of the early church.

   o   Romans – Hebrews, Apostle Paul's letter to the early churches. The church of today still follows suit in many ways. These books also instruct us in how we manage our relationships with our sisters and brothers in Christ.

   o   Genesis – Deuteronomy, the history of the earth and mankind – focusing on the people of Israel.

   o   Joshua – Esther, the historical books of Israel, its wars, judges, prophets and kings. Made for drama wrapped in God's graciousness towards His people.

   o   Job – Song of Solomon, poetry, songs and wisdom literature some written by a man after God's own heart and his son who was the wisest of all.

   o   Isaiah–Malachi, the prophetic books that help us know what happened and gives us a glimpse of what is to happen.

4. **Choose a translation that is easy to follow** but closest to the original text. Download an audible version of the Bible so that you can stay on track when you're on the run.

5. **After your daily reading, reflect on what you've read,** make notes about it or simply reflect on the meaning and what it means for your journey. **Pray to God to help you** in areas that are lacking and thank Him for things that are not.

Red Flag: You have been set up to win in life, but if you do not read the instructions you will surely fail.

.

Day 12: Eating Healthy and Exercising is Important to Your Whole Person

If you've ever wondered why you sometimes feel as bad as you do physically when you feel bad emotionally, you need to know that your body, spirit and soul are one.

Dear friend, I pray that you may enjoy good health and that all may go well with you, even as your soul is getting along well.
—3 John 1:2 NIV

Sister, your body cannot be ignored, when all is well with your soul and especially when all is not. Your body houses your soul and your spirit. Many times, what's going on with your temple (your body) is a direct reflection of what is going on with your soul and your spirit – your soul being the seat of your personality, where decisions are made; the spirit being the part of you that communes with God.

If we eat healthy, will our sinful desires go away? No ma'am. But, according to Stress-management-4-women.com, good nutrition helps to relieve stress. Quite frankly, abstaining from our fleshly desires can be stressful. Stress raises the metabolism level, depletes the body of vitamins and minerals thereby increasing fatigue and becoming more reactive to stressful situations. Eating healthy strengthens the immune system and increases your energy level while lowering the level of stress you experience. Personally, I need all of my strength, all of my will and all of my skill to stay strong. If you catch me sluggish and weary, I'm subject to fall into anything.

If we exercise will our emotional pains go away? Nope. But you've heard of endorphins, right? It's the protein molecules produced by cells in the nervous system that control feelings of stress and frustration. According to Road-to-health.com, endorphins are believed to enhance the immune system, relieve pain and postpone the aging process. Beta-endorphins have the strongest effect on the brain and the body and are released during exercise. It's safe to say that you may be able to manage the stresses of both sinful desires and emotional pain by routinely exercising. Webmd.com says exercise is also good for:

- Controlling weight
- Maintaining healthy bones, muscles and joints
- Reducing risk of high blood pressure, diabetes and heart disease
- Promoting psychological well-being

Here are five easy habits to start without turning your world upside down:

1. Since your body is about 50% water, pour back into yourself. ***Drink at least 64 ounces of water each day*** because your body expels about that much between breathing, sweating and trips to the restroom.
2. ***Eat breakfast each day*** so that your blood sugar level can be stable, enabling you to stay focused and less likely to be irritable.
3. ***Cut back on caffeinated drinks***. Yikes! Not only do they create false highs, but caffeine increases the loss of calcium.
4. ***Reduce and regulate your fried food intake***. Fried foods put you at a higher risk for high blood cholesterol and heart disease.

5. Consider giving your digestive system a day off by setting aside at *least one day a week for fruits and vegetables only*. It won't kill you.

If you're going to start an exercise regime, consider these things first:

1. *See your doctor* for a complete physical. You need to be aware of any restrictions while exercising.
2. Find *a regime that is right for you*. Don't overdue in the beginning; exercise is a progressive activity.
3. *Plan for bad weather days* (exercise you can do inside your home if you can't get to the gym).

Red Flag: You must take care of your spiritual being as well as your physical being. If not, you will not be able to enjoy life to the fullest – single or married. I pray that you will know the importance of the temple God has given you and use it for His glory starting today.

Day 13: You can Minimize Your Flesh

Our bodies are worth more than the flesh we see and the desires that come with it.

And you were dead in the trespasses and sins in which you once walked, following the course of this world, following the prince of the power of the air, the spirit that is now at work in the sons of disobedience – among whom we all once lived in the passions of our flesh, carrying out the desires of the body and the mind, and were by nature children of wrath, like the rest of mankind.
—Ephesians 2: 1-3 ESV

When I was in my twenties, I was convinced my body was my greatest asset. Don't get me wrong, I was well aware of the other attributes God had given me but the physical one got more of my attention; probably because it was the first thing that caught the attention of others.

You'll have to understand that I was one of those skinny teenagers who was pretty much ignored and passed over on the high school dating scene. I was cute and I had pretty hair (which was always disobedient and moved all over my head, much like today). I had a great sense of humor so that helped a little. But for the most part, I was invisible to most young men. I was a late bloomer, but it was cool because I had plenty of good friends who were guys and besides most relationships were maintained by the telephone – not the cell phone but the telephone; remember those?

For the average teenager in the mid 80's there was always someone you met through your cousin's friend. You never saw him because they lived across town, but you were "going together."

So man! When I finally bloomed! Bam! Curves and everything! And oh my goodness, when I learned how to use what I had...it was on! There were many compliments and gifts and commitments – not from me, but from them – and I thought I (or at least one part of me) was better than life itself. In my early twenties, I lived in the clubs, having sexual relationships with whoever I had chemistry with, being sort of care-free – no commitments to anyone. I thought it was acceptable as long as I wasn't really "pushing the envelope" – what I would refer to as going over and above what was usual and customary of any young, single woman. So I thought I was good! I never considered, no less read, what God had to say about the body He had given me, what I was to do with it or not do with it.

It was in my early thirties, after the birth of my fourth child and the emotionally devastating circumstances that came with the pregnancy, that I became sick of the compliments and the gifts and the *lack of* commitment – not from me, but from *them*. Feelings of pain, emptiness and constantly being abandoned pushed me into my first season of abstinence. I was still attractive, but I finally realized that I was more than my flesh and now I wanted others to realize it to. Once I realized how much more I had to offer, I began to see what that really is – the beauty of me and the beauty of the God in me. I am so much more than my flesh. Wrapped in my flesh is love, kindness, generosity, security, joy, laughter, creativity, warmth, compassion, loyalty and the list goes on – all of which deserves to be acknowledged and loved. I am so much more than my flesh. Are you?

Red Flag: You are more than the flesh you see, but it is useful. It is the vessel through which your soul serves the Lord. Therefore, it is imperative that you get a handle on your fleshly desires today. If not, your soul will continue to be driven by them.

Day 14: Hello? You can let "it" go Now!

Now it's time to deal with the real question. While you are unmarried, can you live a life of sexual abstinence, forsaking sex outside of marriage? You know - what God requires of you? THE. ANSWER.IS.YES. Let's look at a few practical ideas to consider and habits to start while you are single. You may not think you can really do this, but I want you to know you can.

There's more to sex than mere skin on skin. Sex is as much spiritual mystery as physical fact. As written in Scripture, "The two become one." Since we want to become spiritually one with the Master, we must not pursue the kind of sex that avoids commitment and intimacy, leaving us more lonely than ever – the kind of sex that can never "become one." There is a sense in which sexual sins are different from all others. In sexual sin we violate the sacredness of our own bodies, these bodies that were made for God-modeled love, for "becoming one" with another. Or didn't you realize that your body is a sacred place, the place of the Holy Spirit? Don't you see that you can't live however you please, squandering what God paid such a high price for? The physical part of you is not some piece of property belonging to the spiritual part of you. God owns the whole works. So let people see God in and through your body.
—I Corinthians 6:16-20 The Message Translation

The act of sex has been trivialized and the power of sex has been underrated. Sex is a connector and every time we treat this act casually, with no strings attached and for the mere physical pleasure of it, we are in fact connecting ourselves to the wrong men for the wrong reason. Sex is a tool that is used for a godly purpose, my sister. When we use this tool for our own purposes, more often than not, we bring about devastating repercussions. Dr. Nicolas Ellen says in his book *"So You Want To Get Married"* that there are three reasons for sex: procreation, pleasure and unity.[1] All three of these belong in the confines of a marriage. When any of them occur outside of the commitment of marriage, somewhere down the line you are sure to have challenges that you have brought on yourself.

You may be thinking, "A challenge is a challenge, what's the difference?" Some challenges in life God allows to come your way to strengthen your walk with Him, to build your character, to grow you. Other challenges in life God uses for discipline in a response to a decision you've made that has drawn you away from Him. In my own life, the former I could walk through a little easier because guilt was not a factor. The latter caused much more pain because I was guilty of sin and most of the 'journey out of pain' was not with God but with myself and others as I fought to justify my feelings and my actions while dealing with the repercussions.

Sexual intimacy is not easy to pull away from, especially if you are in relationship with someone. Three things your abstinence will do in this case: it will test his feelings *for* you; it will test his feelings *about* you; it will test the relationship itself. If you are not romantically involved with someone, this is the perfect time to make a commitment to sexual abstinence. Three things your abstinence will do in this case: it will draw you closer to God; it will give you clarity within yourself and about the man you date; it will strengthen your mind over your body.

---

1 Dr. Nicolas Ellen, *So You Want To Get Married* (Houston: Expository Counseling Center, 2014), Chapter 9

*"All things are lawful for me," but not all things are helpful.
"All things are lawful for me," but I will not be dominated by
anything. "Food is meant for the stomach and the stomach for
food" – and God will destroy both one and the other. The body
is not meant for sexual immorality, but for the Lord, and the
Lord for the body. I Corinthians 6:12-13 ESV*

Red Flag: In this peculiar verse what is in quotations is what
the Apostle Paul repeats from the Corinthians claim; then he
writes an answer. Here's what he's saying: All things are not
helpful though you may have access to it; you should not be
dominated by anything. Things that are not helpful to you, that
do not glorify God in the end, let them go or they will continue
to bring challenges, even misery to your life.

Day 15: You can Quit Before You go to Far!

Know how far you can go before you get there.

But each one is tempted when he is drawn away by his own desires and enticed. Then, when desire has conceived, it gives birth to sin, and sin, when it is full-grown, brings forth death.
—James 1: 14, 15 NKJV

If there is one thing I have learned about sexual abstinence is that sensual desires are not to be played with. Nor are they to be taken for granted. They are strong and powerful, having their own mind. We refer to some parts of our anatomies as if they were a totally separate being with a mind of its own. It would do us good if we recognize that; not giving it power, but giving it credence. When your body is turned on...*it's turned on* and it becomes a formidable contender with the mind.

Here's my "Please excuse me, I have temporarily lost my mind" story:

During my twenties, as I mentioned before, my relationships were more casual in nature. Occasionally there would be sexual intimacy – no commitment, no true desire to marry, just hanging out. When I would get "caught up" in these intimate moments with *whoever,* I threw all senses out of the window and just went with whatever my body was feeling at the time. Here's what's crazier than that: there would be times when in the middle of the moment the feeling left but because I started the act, the only thing I heard in my mind was "might as well finish it." *I wonder who that was saying that?*

As I began to grow spiritually, there were times when the intimate moments were deliberate and very heated, but the Lord was dealing with me. The words in my mind then changed to "you know you shouldn't but since you started, go ahead and finish it." *And who was saying that, I wonder?*

Finally, I learned that it's okay to say "I don't want to do this" at *any time* and get up and walk away from the situation. There is no "point of no return". You can always return.

You can actually be in a very compromising position and snap. Just say:

"Please excuse me, I have temporarily lost my mind. Pardon me as I reach over you to get that and put that back on. Thank you."

I don't care if garments are hanging from the ceiling fan, when the Holy Spirit convicts you (and He won't be late); quit! And whoever you are with, should respect that or you may have a larger problem than abstaining.

I remember the night I first decided to quit, that is – to quit lending pieces of myself to those who could not honor me before God for whatever reason. I decided to quit sharing intimate moments with someone who would tip out in the middle of the night. I decided to quit hearing the words "I'll call you when I get home" because home should have been with me. I remember laying there in my void soul, watching as he walked out of the door – his silhouette in the moon light from the bay window of my bedroom.

I could feel parts of me drifting out of my soul- jumping into his pocket, into his jacket, into the palm of his hand. And there he was, walking out of the door with it. No obligation to ever turn back. Did he call when he got home? Yes. He was a great guy and he loved me, but I was alone. I hated that feeling so much. It was worse than any self-inflicted pain I had ever felt. Over thirty years old, four children, single parent and I just quit. That night, I had gone too far but it wouldn't happen again for years.

Our lives are filled with quotes about not quitting. On the contrary, the Bible teaches that there is a time to quit; life even teaches that. When you're going in the wrong direction away from God's purpose and plan you can always quit before you go too far. So where is "too far?" Too far is where you find yourself after the intimate act is done and though your body may feel temporarily satisfied, your spirit is void because you're back at square one – defeated by your body with the mind of its own because you did not use the power God gave you to simply quit.

Red Flag: Don't keep pushing the envelope. Set boundaries for yourself. Self-discipline is so much better than having discipline imposed on you. I pray that you will come to know how far is too far.

Day 16: You can Guard Your Eyes and Your Ears

Know that what you see and what you hear has direct impact on your thoughts.

Keep your heart with all vigilance, for from it flow the springs of life.
—Proverbs 4:23 ESV

Sister, some things that are in your "line of sight" or an "earshot away" can actually be harmful to you, especially if you are aiming to please God.

First things first – you may be asking what is in my "line of sight." You're not someone who frequents adult entertainment. But it's more than rated X productions that pull your attention towards intimacy. The world has so much more romanticism to offer and I don't mean sexuality. I mean romanticism. We live in a world full of romantic ideals – the American dream, banker hours, soul mates, etc. We find solace in happily ever after and long, lost loves reuniting. There's nothing wrong with that sort of imagery through entertainment but sometimes we slip so far into what we see that we compare our lives to and gradually start longing for the romantic ideal that is not immediately in our grasp.

Music lovers will agree that music is a part of our daily lives. It is present when we commute, when we work, when we socialize, when we worship, when we celebrate, when we do our weekly chores around the house and other times that are particular and significant. When we have the opportunity to actually hear the lyrics we are not outputting or talking but we are receiving input or listening. So the words we hear recall or perhaps introduce thoughts relative to what's being said. Suddenly the music becomes the soundtrack to the video being replayed or produced in our minds. It's a replay if it is a memory of someone we've been with. It's a production if we're processing thoughts about being with someone in the future. Do you agree?

There is no shame in watching a romantic movie or listening to your favorite songs, fantasizing about your experiences with love, recalling fond memories. Even anticipating the new memories you'll make is normal and natural. But if you find yourself drifting from the screen and asking "why not me?" then change the channel. Media is created to entertain and take your mind away from some realities, if only for a short time. But it can also take your mind to a place that is empty, lacking or lonely. If entertainment ever does that, it's best to change the channel. If what you are watching or hearing takes you to any place that the Lord is not, simply change the channel or turn it off.

Emptiness and longing for what you do not have can cause one to be bitter and bitterness can set in the heart of a woman. Sorrow can set in the heart of a woman. Know that you have a responsibility to keep your heart pure before the Lord; so anything that is not a benefit to see or hear can actually be a detriment. Negativity can make its way into your soul. While media can be positive in some settings, it can also be detriment when you're in a lonely space in your life. It would be wise to choose what to see and what to hear.

In addition to this, be mindful of what information you receive by way of artist who have no desire to please your Father. Know that every artist has a view of God, of creation, of purpose and of eternity. Their worldview may not align with yours, but you may find yourself repeating exactly what you *do not* believe because you like the beat. You may find yourself buying into an ungodly idea that you support by simply tuning in because you think it's funny, or interesting to watch. It would be wise to choose what to see and what to hear.

Red Flag: The media is a powerful tool. It is not just for entertainment, but it is for messaging. My prayer for you is that you choose wisely what message you will receive today – one of wholeness or one that tears at your heart and/or your mind.

Day 17: Loneliness is a Real Thing

I want you to know the pain of loneliness is real and you are not the only one who feels this way.

"Turn to me and be gracious to me, for I am lonely and afflicted. The troubles of my heart are enlarged; bring me out of my distresses. "
—Psalm 25: 16, 17 NASB 2020

Loneliness can be defined as a feeling of sadness when one is socially isolated; but I've come to know that we can be lonely in a room full of people, laughter filling each space from wall to wall. Let me submit that loneliness is the feeling of sadness when one is intimately isolated – when there is no one to share love and life with.

Loneliness can be overwhelming, especially when you have decided against wasting time with "place holders" – men who hold the place until your husband gets here. You know the place –

The place of the male voice that whispers sweet things in your ears or responds to your talk about your job, or your friends, or your mother.

The place of the male dominance that guides you by taking your hand as he leads you across the busy street or lets you out in front of the movie theatre, before he parks the car.

The place of the male role that looks at your car when you swore you heard a knock in the engine or when he picks up the check at your favorite restaurant.

The place of the male strength when he holds you in his arms because you're cold, or afraid, or hurt, or happy, or lonely.

For the most part, those of us who have been at this single life for a while learn to fill our days with constructive busyness but at the end of the day when all of our friends have gone home (sometimes to their husbands) and all of the work is done and the kids have gone to bed, when the last person at the church gives you a hug and goes to their car – loneliness presents itself, dressed for bed because it's going to settle in and stay the night.

Unless you've experienced loneliness, you may not know its power; but for those of us who do, we acknowledge that it is real; it is formidable. But here's the good news, if you struggle with it long enough, if you bring Christ in on the battle, every day you will get a little stronger. You learn that loneliness can be a temporary feeling that goes away as quickly as it comes. You learn that you can ask God to take your mind off of it and He will. You learn how to be alone and not be lonely. You will learn how to trust God with your feelings. You learn how to say no to "place holders" when you're at your loneliness because you recognize the red flag, the danger in getting too close to the wrong man for the right reason.

The right reason? Remember, my dear sister, that God made you *for* man (Genesis 2:18). It is quite natural to have a desire to be married, to give your husband children, to nurture a family. It is almost out of style for a woman to confess that she desires a family to care for. It is as if in this day of liberation and equality, the woman whose primary focus is the daily care for her family is an anomaly.

You're a super woman if you are able to balance your career, ready-made meals or fast food schedules, your children's social and athletic calendar, your duties at church, with your sorority and the homeowner's association. But if your day starts at 6 am with a full breakfast for your husband and children, packing healthy lunches for all, driving the car pool to school, picking up your husband's dry-cleaned shirts, grocery shopping, lugging them in the house and putting them away, volunteering at school lunch time, swinging by the pharmacy, putting on a load of clothes before starting dinner, picking the children up from school, giving them a snack, helping with homework, serving the dinner, spending time with the children watching family TV or maybe a weeknight Bible study, cleaning the kitchen after turning over the clothes and finally going to bed only to be tapped on the shoulder by your husband – then you're just a lowly homemaker who needs to get a life.

It is a good thing to desire a husband and a family. It is okay to feel lonely without this; but remember in your wait that you are not alone. God sees you, He sees your heart, He hears your desires and He will answer.

Red Flag: Be aware of your feelings of loneliness but don't let the thoughts that come with it overwhelm you. I pray that you will find fulfillment in life starting today; fulfillment that will sustain you until you begin to share your life with someone else. I pray your mate will find you content, not lacking anything, that your union will not be one born out of desperation, but out of devotion to God and to one another.

Day 18: A Little Something Else I Need You to Know

I want you to move beyond the pity party.

**My father, who has given them to me, is greater than all…
—John 10:29 NASB 2020**

Many times in our wait, we withdraw. We do not withdraw from others, from our jobs, from our daily rituals or even our church activities but we withdraw from God. We may not realize we are in "wait." We think we are in "refusal." In our minds, God has refused to grant us our deliverance, our healing or our heart's desire, for whatever reason. And so we withdraw from the very One who holds life and death in the palm of His hand. By life I mean a heart of joy and by death, I mean a mind of anguish.

Sometimes we grow so weary of disguise, disappointment, disagreement and disgust that we see no Light in so much darkness, no Redeemer in so much loss, no Healer in so much emotional sickness. And we withdraw.

We stop feeding our spiritual beings hoping it will quietly starve and die. Spiritual growth can hurt. Spiritual maturity sometimes cost spiritual pain. Who wants pain? We decide that God's love or His promises are not for us but for everyone else. We decide to live a life void of personal worship, prayer and righteousness. Does it matter? Everything in us feels that it does not.

For the person who has never been in the hand of God living like this will be okay. But Jesus says this:

My sheep hear my voice, and I know them, and they follow me. I give them eternal life, and they will never perish and no one will snatch them out of my hand. My father, who has given them to me, is greater than all, and no one is able to snatch them out of the Father's hand. John 10:27-29 ESV

So here's the thing – if Christ is your Savior, if you are truly His sheep, you are in His hand. No one, not even you yourself, can snatch you out. So fall on the floor, scream and shout if you must. You may even decide to take all of your toys and go home (withdraw) but at the end of the day you are still in His hand. He is still God and you are still His child. So when you find yourself about to withdraw, work that mess out and get back in the game because His Father who has sent Him is greater than all – all of your disappointments, all of your pain and all of your self-pity.

xoxo
Now let's continue....

Red Flag: Not being able to see God clearly as He works in your life can cause you to want to abandon your faith in Him. This is a trick of the mind. Do not fall for it. You still belong to God, whether you can track Him or not.

Day 19: Know who You are in Christ

Know that we are valuable to God; we must know our worth to Him and to our world.

For You have made him a little lower than the angels, and You have crowned him with glory and honor.
—Psalm 8:5 NKJV

Sometimes I think we forget who we really are. We are the most intelligent design of the Creator of the universe. We are made in His image, in His likeness (Genesis 1:26). Many of the characteristics that God has we have some degree of. Off the cuff, here are a few I can think of. We have dominion, creativity, the ability to love, intellect and compassion. God has poured so much of Himself into each of us; then He gave His best in the person of Jesus Christ so that we may be reconciled to Him and taught how to live out His best. In addition, He gave Himself, again, in the person of the Holy Spirit so that we may be empowered to do so.

So why can't that happen? Why aren't we able to naturally live out the wonderful qualities God has placed in us? What hinders us from being the very best we can be? Sometimes it has to do with our self-esteem or how we perceive ourselves. So where does this low opinion of "me" come from? Perhaps it was some sort of neglect or abuse. Perhaps it came from an inability to meet someone else's standards. Has this happened to you? Maybe someone in your close circle had an emotional problem but you were the recipient of their frustration or their anger. Perhaps there was no praise, no warmth, no interest in who you were. Or were you the odd one out at home or at school?

So here we are, fully grown, and whatever happened in the past still drives our future. We were unable to understand the shortcomings of others – their pride or insecurities, hatefulness or the like. Whatever negative impact we experienced in our childhood may still have much power over our thoughts, our decision-making and our behaviors to this day.

The regulated acceptance of these emotional offenses may cause us to readily accept the emotional offense of others, even after we become adults, as if it were usual and customary to be devalued. We may even accept the notion that this type of behavior is justified by our inability to please the offender, never considering that their own pain causes dissatisfaction in their own souls.

Let's visit Genesis 1: 21, 24 and then 26. There is no other creature on earth that distinctly represents God's image other than mankind. Every other thing God made is uniquely its own. But with us, God has chosen to share His likeness. Am I saying that God has four limbs, an upright spine, ten fingers and toes? I do not know but I do know that separate from every other thing mentioned in His creative genius, in mankind He has chosen to see His reflection.

Consider this, you were uniquely designed for a purpose in life that only you can fulfill. Whether it is the place you hold in your family, in your friend circle or just in day-to-day life, it is uniquely your place. No one has the footprint, the life experiences, the exact feelings, the exact expressions in life that you do. Look around you and the joy you bring to others. Their life is complete because of you.

So, no matter your skin tone, the length of your hair or lack thereof; no matter the width of your nose or the size of your lips or hips or buttocks that leave the room last when you walk out, you are a reflection of our beautiful God. That's how God sees you, that's how you should see others and certainly that's how you should see yourself.

Red Flag: Know your worth to God and to mankind starting today. You are uniquely made; you are an asset to our world. Low self-esteem attracts the wrong friends and the wrong mates. Feeling good about who you are looks good on you and sends the message "I like me." I pray that, starting today, you will wear the beauty that God gave you well.

Day 20: Know how to Participate in Your Life

Singleness can be for an appointed period in life but is always for an appointed purpose in life.

The thief comes only to steal and kill and destroy; I have come that they may have life, and have it to the full.
—John 10:10 NIV

The first few months I abstained from premarital sex, girlfriend, my body was screaming at me! "What is going on? Where is he?" All of the practices I have so far written to you, I, too, was practicing. All of that was fine and good but I had all of this "new energy" that I didn't know what to do with.

Two things I want you to know. First, that nagging feeling you have in your mid-section will leave; it will come back and leave again. This may go on for a while until the frequency decreases. Two words – cold showers. Secondly, you must intentionally refocus your mind on other fulfilling activities in life. Understand that our bodies didn't develop sexual desires overnight nor will they go away overnight. But, because you are training your body to yield its desires to your mind, you must be intentional and decisive about what to do with your new energy.

If you are in a committed relationship that has been strained because of your decision, you may be contemplating if the relationship can withstand this change. If you were only casually dating and having casual sex, you may be feeling lonely because those relationships, though casual, seemed to fill a void. If you were not involved with anyone at all, you may toss and turn at night wondering if God is seeing your new approach to wholeness, if there will be a change in your future relationships and will He reward your faithfulness. So, let's get your mind focused on something else. Hobbies are good, but at this point, you really need something in which your self-worth can be validated. It is important to know that you are needed and wanted in places other than behind closed doors.

There are three things you can do:
Something for God *and/or*
Something for others *and/or*
Something for yourself

Perhaps you are working within your church family. If you are not, I encourage you to begin immediately (See 1 Corinthians 12:4-7). However, there are other faith-based organizations that are always in need of help. A benefit to working in this type of community is the exposure to a diversity of believers who will come together in collaborating resources for one cause. Here's an example: if you are a "pro-lifer", consider volunteering in a crisis pregnancy center. There is no requirement of personal experience in a specific area in order to volunteer your services.

"Find out where God is working and join Him."
—Henry T. Blackaby

In the year 2020 some of us may have witnessed more loss in one year than many will witness over their lifetime. The COVID 19 pandemic hit the United States and seized social lives, livelihoods, material possessions, good health and worse of all – lives of our loved ones. Every community has an organization whose primary goal is to minister to those in need of basic necessities. Get involved. Even before the pandemic, there was the homeless and the hungry. Looking into the faces of those who experience challenges like these gives you a new window into your own life. Hearing their stories open a new sound to your own heart. It may beat to a rhythm you never knew existed. Suddenly, the lack that seems so huge in your own life is reduced to its appropriate size.

> "For I was hungry and you gave Me food, I was thirsty and you gave Me drink, I was a stranger and you welcomed Me, I was naked and you clothed Me, I was sick and you visited Me, I was in prison and you came to Me."
> **—Matthew 25: 35-36 NKJV**

Consider doing something for you. This may sound selfish, but it is not. This is a time to explore new styles and expand what is already great. Get busy re-inventing you! Do something you've always wanted to do but for whatever reason, you just didn't do it. Learn a new language, go back to school. Either take courses towards an unfinished degree or leisure learning. Building upon the gifts that God has placed in you will always enable you to do something great for God and others.

> "No matter who you are, no matter what you did, no matter where you've come from, you can always change, become a better version of yourself."
> **—Madonna**

Red Flag: You must participate in your life at every stage, in every season starting today. Do not sit on the sidelines of your life watching the days goes by. Embrace every day as a gift of time, especially in your singleness. If not, you will only have some old version of you to present to your future husband. What he will want is a brand new you, birthed from the springtime of your life.

Day 21: You Don't Always Have to Know

"If I see God moving, but then I don't…what should I do? The answer is WAIT! You will soon see what He is doing.

And Moses said unto the people, Fear ye not, stand still, and see the salvation of the LORD, which he will shew to you today: for the Egyptians whom ye have seen to day, ye shall see them again no more for ever.
—Exodus 14:13 KJV

We are truly a culture of "instant". We want everything right now. Everything is urgent. "The quicker, the better" is our motto. Instant Grits. Instant success. Instagram.

Do you know that's how we are with God, too? How many times have we struggled with waiting for God to answer, waiting for God to move – move something or move someone?

Waiting on God is different than waiting on anyone or anything else. There's no true way to actually know what's going on. No way to check progress. There's no attendant you can pull to the side and ask "How much longer?" There's no timer, no countdown to answered prayer.

Once the Lord had me at the "wait station" for years. During my wait, someone asked me "You got any wait in you?" I think I said no, if I answered at all because I truly did not. Even though the Lord assured me He had it under control, I still wanted to know when – when are you going to bring it to pass? When will the pain stop? At times I didn't see any evidence of Him working. I either dismissed it all together or tried to bring the solutions to fruition myself (that may not be you though). I've made many mistakes when I took hold of my own solution. In my impatience I intervened in whatever God was doing and I may have changed the trajectory of the situation; I will never know for sure. What I do know for sure is that I said something in haste, or did something in selfishness because I wanted resolution, and quickly. Two things I learned: God reveals what He is doing on a "need to know" basis and my "need to be in the loop" was not important at all. To this day, I continue to wonder what would have happened if I had kept my mouth closed and my hands out of God's business.

I learned to wait after constant interference and interrupting in places I had no business, under the guise of trying to help God but I was actually only trying to help myself. In my wait for something to happen *for* me, something else was happening *in* me. I was growing, being developed in areas of my life that was stagnant. Within every painful, hopeless, heartbreaking circumstance there were places that God grew me. He used times of turmoil and strife to grow me up in Him. It was the natural growth process taking place – some things had to die so that some things greater could live.

As I waited to see what would happen, I came to know Him better. I came to know Him as a friend who was constantly looking out for me though I thought no one was in my corner. I learned how to be a better friend to Him. I opened up to Him and confided all of my thoughts about being alone, being lonely, being single all of my life; not being financially secure. Then I listened to His thoughts and I began to see how His way was better for me. I came to respect His point of view. Though I may not have agreed with it, I was willing to give it a try. That's what real friends do.

Now there were a few times when I needed to know that He was still working on my concerns and He was gracious to allow me to see His hands on my life. So, then I returned the favor and allowed Him to work in peace, if you will – no more interruptions from me, no progress checks, no "going over the plan one more time." Over time, I began to trust that He has it – my past, my present, my future and all. See what happened to me?

Red Flag: Be patient while He works on your behalf starting today. Settle your spirit so that you will not deter the blessings He has in store for you. Moreover, let the work He does *in* you have its way. I am praying for you.

Day 22: We Learn From our Mistakes, we Just Don't Make Them

Know that we must actively learn from our mistakes, not just make them and move on.

Good and upright is the LORD; therefore he instructs sinners in the way. He leads the humble in what is right, and teaches the humble his way.
—Psalm 25:8, 9 ESV

We've been looking at ourselves. Let's look at someone else for a change.

I have a friend, whom I love dearly. I've known him for over 20 years now and for almost 20 years I have been watching him go through the same thing over and over again. Ever see the movie "50 First Dates"? If you have, then you get the concept. Except this guy does not have short-term memory loss though he may act as if he does. I'm not saying he goes through similar experiences or closely related experiences. I'm telling you he goes through the same thing, over and over and over again and it's been over 20 years I said! He makes the same choice, lives that choice out the same way and reaps the very same consequence, over and over again. Not only that, but he takes his entire family on this merry-go-round that is his life.

I, too, rode with him on his merry-go-round. It took a real toll on me. I was dizzy and breaking the bank trying to get him out of this cycle. Then someone asked me "Penny, why are you so stressed out, wanting something for them that they don't want for themselves?" At that very moment, a light came on and I was able to get off the merry-go-round that is my friend's life. I joined his friends and family members who love him as well as I do, and just watched him go round and round while others choose to go from one destination to the next.

And isn't it a choice? What we do with life's experiences? Do we take the hits and ignore the lessons being taught? Or do we make some attempt to seek the lessons of life and apply them in order to get different outcomes as we grow and move from destination to destination? "Some people just don't get it," another friend has said about my friend's situation, "if you continue to get the same result, when will you ever learn to do something different?" Good question.

There are different levels of learning: Rote, recognition, restatement, relation and realization. When you come to the realization level, you realize a new idea is better than your old idea and you begin to act according to what you've learned. It is real to you – the consequences and the result of what is set into motion. You are now ready to change your behavior patterns.

All through life you have been learning, moving in and out of life's experiences – sometimes shuffling, sometimes gliding, sometimes strolling, sometimes walking, sometimes crawling. Was it all in vain or did you embrace the valuable lesson that God was teaching you for that moment in time? Did you experience the "ah ha" moment? Did you make a change? Or did you miss it all together?

Have you missed a chance to get to know God in a different way, maybe even better? Were you able to see yourself as you really are or someone else as they are and make a better decision about where they belong in your life? Or are you still moving in and out of the same experiences – shuffling, gliding, strolling, walking but mostly crawling?

At some point, we must actively learn from our mistakes. What do I mean by actively learning? This is when you acknowledge the mistakes, misjudgments or misappropriations that caused you or someone else pain, repent, ask for forgiveness, take heed to the lessons in them and help others to avoid to them.

Red Flag: Embrace the new wisdoms birthed from your mistakes in order to make changes in your thought processes and behavior patterns starting today. I pray that you move from one destination to the other. God forbid that at the end of your days, your life would have only been a merry-go-round.

Some Things
to Know
Concerning
Others!

Day 23: Taming Your Touch, Your Talk and Your Technology—Knowing How to Communicate in a way That Won't Come Back to Bite You

You need to know that how you communicate can help or hinder your efforts to maintain abstinence.

But the fruit of the Spirit is love, joy, peace, forbearance,
kindness, gentleness and self-control.
Against such things there is no law.
—Galatians 5: 22-23 NIV

Flirting has gone to a whole new level! I was once told my flirtation was outdated. Gone are the days of a subtle smile or overzealous laughter at a man's jokes. No more gentle kisses on the cheek at the end of the evening. No more "I'm cooking a roast on Sunday, want to come over after church?" Today, those gestures mean little or nothing at all to most people.

How we communicate our thoughts have drastically changed, and it appears roles have been switched. Men are the hunted and women are the hunters! How's that for women's lib? Thirty years ago, the only way a woman could be a tease was in person. Back in the day, the most you could do at a distance was talk dirty over the phone but today you can "*show and tell*" from across the globe. Understand that I'm not talking about pornography. That's a totally different issue. I'm talking about how we communicate our desires to Gary Goodjob. Sure, it can be fun and it can keep the interest going but does it help our quest for righteous living? What if your teasing gets out of hand?

You may ask "what's wrong with touching?" It's not the issue of touching others, but it is the issue of *how* you touch others. You may not think anything of it, but this quote has come up in a few blogs by researchers: "Momentary touches, the experts say – whether an exuberant high five, a warm hand on the shoulder, or a creepy touch to the arm – can communicate an even wider range of emotions than gestures or expressions, and sometimes do so more quickly and accurately than words."

It's not only the touch itself but it's where you touch that determines the message to be received. Even though this communication can occur mindlessly, accidentally and innocently, if done consistently it can create an atmosphere that may not work if you're trying to abstain from sex. If you're a "touchy-feely" person, be mindful of how and where you touch William Wavyhair. Sometimes the simple touch of "I care" or "I like you" can be misinterpreted as "I'm ready", so tame your touch.

The same is true with your conversation, your talk. I mean, it's fun when you say a little something, then he piggybacks on that and you give a snappy comeback on what he said and there you go – your mind begins to travel places that you have no business visiting. When you're not mindful of your conversations, the enemy is sure to show up, especially when your guard is down in relaxing, intimate exchanges. Once you get on a certain subject, one that is enticing and intriguing, your focus is set on that thought. If your mind stays there too long, your body is aroused and is soon to chase after your thoughts. Make sense? While you might want Henry Handsome to know you're attracted to him, you don't want him to think you're ready for something more, if you're really not ready.

Now here's an issue we certainly didn't have thirty years ago – cell phones and social media – what you type and what you show. Need I say more? What if that text or that picture you sent to excite someone ends up in the wrong hands? It happens all of the time. Have you ever had a picture from years ago (that you forgot you took or received) drop out of "the cloud" when you didn't ask it to?

For those in public arenas this kind of mistake brings about public humiliation. But what about you? Whether you are a public figure or not, are you concerned about your private integrity (what you say to yourself about your actions) while you are posting sexually oriented messages on social media?

There are many things in our lives that we cannot control but there are many things we can – like how we present ourselves and how we govern ourselves. Following Christ calls for self-control. As Christians enjoy the fascinating experience of change in the way the world operates, we should practice self-control even more. No matter what new ways to communicate trend, the believer's trend stays the same – representing God in all that we say and do.

Red Flag: You should seriously consider how and what you communicate beginning today. You cannot speak one way of life and desire another. I pray that all of your communication, moving forward, will honor God.

Day 24: You are in Charge of You. Regulating the Date

Your chances for success in abstaining will be greater if you intentionally plan your dates.

Therefore, whether you eat or drink, or whatever you do, do all to the glory of God.
— I Corinthians 10: 31 NKJV

Are you kidding? You had to know it would come to this! How can you do something intentionally without proper planning, proper preparations? Sure, many people just plunge right in, but God is an orderly God. He's methodical and meticulous. He didn't just throw the earth together, nor the heavens, nor anything, nor anyone who dwells in either of them. He doesn't even throw circumstances and situations together.

> Stay with me, my sister. We are in the middle of answering the question "Can I maintain sexual abstinence?" Here's what you should know. Sexual abstinence, obeying Scripture as it pertains to the body God gave you, is His way of protecting you and preserving you. Remember, the fence is there for *your* protection.

The very words you're reading were not thrown together. Many growth spurts, many pains and many joys had to be experienced before the words got here. Severe disciplinary actions had been taken towards the writer so that you may somehow be assured that God is looking out for you. The words are written with much transparency, much admonition and much love. I hope you feel all three. He did not throw this exhortation together for you. If you're serious about dedicating your whole self to God, making every effort to abide by His rules for your life, you're going to have to give some serious thought to how you're going to live this thing out. You've gotten some advice on daily practices like devotion, exercising and eating healthier, but what about your dating practices? Let's go back to the basics and ask who, what, why and when.

We have the *what* – we're talking about dating. Now *why* date? Of course, the most obvious reason is to marry Peter Perfection. But what if you're not quite ready for marriage yet? Maybe there's a recent divorce or worse, a recent death of a spouse or even worse – your credit score is like 35 (all good reasons in my opinion). You may want to date for companionship. But did you read with Gary Chapman said about reasons for dating? Perhaps you have not considered these, but they are definitely worth looking at.

1. You should date to get to know members of the opposite sex in an effort to relate to them as individual people. Getting to know others is instrumental if you're going to serve others. See 1 Corinthians 9:19.
2. In dating you learn names, personalities and philosophies – the qualities of personhood.
3. In dating you are able to see your own strengths and weaknesses.
4. Dating affords you an opportunity to serve others.
5. Dating will help you to discover the *kind* of person you are to marry. [1]

Who should you date? Consider your relationship with God first, then consider what type of person would complement

_____
1 Gary Chapman, *The Five Love Languages – Singles Edition* (Chicago: Northfield Publishing, 2009) 148-153

that relationship, not hinder it. It bears repeating: *Consider your relationship with God first, then consider what type of person would complement that relationship, not hinder it.* Many great women of God have fallen because they did not consider.

Now you can consider pretty simple things like **when** you will date. What is an appropriate hour to be on a date? Some people have a mindset to "work" Monday through Thursday, live life at 100% Friday and Saturday, then worship at 100% on Sunday morning. Sunday evening is the time to get ready for the work week. What is the best day of the week for *you* to date? If you're living life at 100% on Fridays and Saturdays, giving it everything you have, aiming to get all you can from it, you may need to date on Tuesdays. Not only when but **where** will you date? Are romantic dinners off the beaten path or long walks on the beach always the best idea? Will you always ride together, or should there be times when you meet out? A single ride to the next destination gives you time to think before you act.

Consider these questions: What will you wear or not wear? What will you eat, drink or not eat and not drink? If you chose to drink an adult beverage, what is your limit before your clear head becomes cloudy? *"Drinking makes you forget your responsibilities, and you mistreat the poor."* Proverbs 31:5 CEV Just so you know.

It's okay to plan for the best outcome. I would say that you would be more successful if you planned not to fail as you are empowered by the Holy Spirit in your efforts not to do so.

Red Flag: Use your head in your social life. Plan for success in maintaining abstinence. I pray that you won't just "go with the flow" beginning today. The flow can lead you down dark roads of regret, of despair and dark roads of isolation.

Day 25: What to do About Those Comments and Questions—Brushing and Moving

If you're tired of people being insensitive about your singleness and you're wondering what else you can do besides slap them, the answer is: Brush it off and keep it moving.

Good sense makes one slow to anger, and it is his glory to overlook an offense.
—Proverbs 19:11 ESV

What has always accompanied a woman's singleness are the comments she gets about it – at family holidays, at her married girlfriend's BBQ, at the church picnic and wherever else she ventures to go alone. If she shows up with a male friend at any of the aforementioned gatherings, she has to publish a disclaimer stating "This is just a friend" or the man will be sized up, interviewed and fitted for a tux before that evening is over. This may be true in some cases for a man but probably not; he'll have protection from his married male counterparts who vicariously live through him.

Sometimes the words may not be spoken, but the look of pity may speak volumes. It's the look that says "Bless her heart, she doesn't have anybody. What a shame; but she's a pretty girl." Or maybe it's the look that wonders "Why is she eating alone? What's wrong with her?" Sometimes, there are no words or looks but she may feel the awkwardness, maybe because she is asking those same questions, making those same comments to herself – about herself.

These questions and comments seem to never cease fire. They may die down after a few times of "I don't know" or "I'm waiting on the Lord," but just as sure as bad debt and unwanted hairs, they resurface. When I was single, almost a year went by before I enjoyed the company of my family. Maybe there were comments or maybe there weren't, but I felt out of place, even though a few family members were unmarried – very few. Holidays were quick drop-ins and any other gatherings were quick drive-bys. It had become too painful to watch everybody have somebody – except for me. Can you relate?

It didn't take long for me to grow less tolerable of the comments and the questions – verbal or otherwise. I resolved that it was okay to pass on a few events if I wasn't up for the challenge that day. I pulled closer to the few single friends I had instead of spending so much time with married couples. At one point, the only single friend I had was me.

But I also had to learn how to make peace with my feelings about being unmarried – whether it was disappointment, pain or loneliness. I had to learn how to respond to others in those moments; I couldn't be on an island by myself forever. The first thing I reconciled is people who love me don't come from a place of malice but from a place of concern and *ignorance*. Yes, ignorance. They were probably unaware of what I was feeling and/or the awkwardness of the moment when they made comments about my singleness. They may not have known how sensitive the subject was for me. For this reason, I overlooked the offense.

I had to find ways to turn the conversation into a light-hearted exchange. I'd joke about it, at first pretending that I was okay with being alone. Then suddenly, I became okay with being alone because I became content. I was able to brush it off and keep it moving.

Then there were the "church people" who prophesied when *he* would come, who *he* would be and what *he* would be wearing when I met him. No offense taken. They meant well and they may have truly believed they heard from God. I thanked them and loved them because it meant my burden was on their heart. They had been thinking of me and perhaps praying for me. After about the third "The Lord told me to tell you…." I brushed it off and kept it moving because all three 'prophecies' were different.

Finally, there were people who just wanted to be ugly, wanted to remind me that I was alone and at one point lonely. They were willing to be used by the enemy to shame me and knowingly aimed to hurt my feelings. It took me a while, but I took no offense when I realized that we don't fight against flesh and blood but rulers, authorities and wickedness in high places (Ephesians 6:12). It was the power of the Holy Spirit that allowed me to brush it off and keep it moving.

Red Flag: Know that side comments and direct questions will come. Be prepared for them. I pray that you will remember my observations and consider them yourself. May your heart move from a sunken place to a place of power in order to brush it off and keep it moving.

Day 26: Figuring out True Friendship

Have you ever wondered why relationships fail? Being single, you've thought about romantic relationships that fail; but have you ever considered the failure of friendships? What you need to know is that people rarely see others for who they are, but they look at them according to who they want them to be.

A friend loves at all times, and a brother is born for adversity.
—Proverbs 17:17 ESV

One of the worst things any company can do is put the wrong person in the wrong position. Have you ever had a manager who was not only unqualified for his/her position but had not earned the right to be there? Somehow, they just slipped into the position without anyone even knowing who they were or where they came from. Later on, you found out that they either knew somebody at the top (who was just as unscrupulous as they were) or that they were slick talkers who presented themselves as well qualified and able to handle the responsibility. Not! Eventually the entire department took an unnecessary hit, and it took months and unprecedented borrowed resources to recover from it.

This same misappropriation can happen in your personal life. You appoint someone who is unqualified and undeserved to fill a position in your life that only few should be entitled to – the position of friend. Before you know it, that same unqualified and undeserved person is promoted to a more intimate level, a closer position. Time goes by and you begin to realize how unfit they are for that position. It was a misappropriation and because your life is an entity that produces services and goods for those around you, it took some time, maybe some borrowed resources to make up for the hit you took because you put the wrong person in the wrong position. The person who was there for a "reason" or a "season" was somehow bumped to the "lifetime" slot with no formal training, no orientation to the position and no experience in the daily operations of you. They were not able to perform the required duties, sometimes not even at the fundamental level, yet they slipped into a position of authority (they dictate how you respond to other areas in your life) and a position of control (they sometimes regulate how you feel from day to day).

A friend of mine once said "When you first meet a potential mate, they should interview for that position for about 12 months. You shouldn't invest any emotion into the interview period." What did he mean by that? Spending more time in conversational exchange? Really listening to his thought processes, his views on life, family, love and God? Purposefully watching his interaction with his family, close friends, strangers and enemies? Examining how he handles his faith, loss, anger, truth, deceit, adversities, abundance, lack and everything else life throws at him from day to day?

All this we need to have some knowledge of before we deem a person a "friend"? Absolutely! We sprinkle out the word "friend" like cold water on a cool day…I said a *cool day*, meaning it's not necessarily a need, but it's more of a want. We open ourselves to those we ultimately have nothing in common with. We open ourselves to people who may not have our best interest at heart. At times, we allow them to bring us down to a level God never intended us to be. We should move towards making decisions about our friends with our heads and not our hearts. Our associates are chosen for us through the affiliations we chose. Our acquaintances are chosen by the circles we are drawn to; but we hand pick our friends and sometimes too hastily and too loosely.

My friend said we should not get emotionally involved during "the interview process." I wish it were that easy. Sometimes you cross paths with someone and there is so much chemistry between you two. You really click with him and you feel like you've been knowing him all of your life. Stop! You have NOT. Be patient and get to know him. Calm your heart and your hormones, if need be. Take time for fellowship before friendship.

Place friendship on a higher shelf than it may have been. Make space for acquaintances and associates right beneath. Decide the most effect ways to move people from an inappropriate slot to a slot that best fit them and who they are, not who you want them to be. This may mean you pull away from them, still loving them but quietly shifting their responsibilities in your life. Don't allow them to be responsible for your confidence or your trust. Quietly shift your time and your attention. Allow God to direct your reorganization. He will tell you what to say and when to say to any and everyone.

Your friendship is too precious. It opens the door to your heart. If you've experienced heartache of any kind before, you will know that your heart must be protected (Proverbs 4:23). A friend protects your heart, intentionally and by default.

Red Flag: RE-examine your inner circle. Consider what God says about friendship in Proverbs 27:17. Do your friends sharpen you? Consider Psalm 1:1. Are you walking, standing or sitting with the ungodly? I pray that you allow Him to show you how to be a friend, how to choose friends and how to manage friendships starting today.

Now Back
to You!

Day 27: The Factor is You

Know that you are the most determining factor in the success of your your singleness.

**"...The LORD is with thee, thou mighty man of valour."
—Judges 6:12 KJV**

Some would argue that we avoid taking responsibility for what we've done in the past and for our part in our future. Some walk through life as if they are absolutely powerless, shifting blame of negative outcomes in their lives on outside forces - their childhood, their income or lack of, their bad relationships – never accepting responsibility for the decisions they make.

You need to know that the difference between your past and your future is *you*. Be prepared to be different moving forward. By now, you have either gained new knowledge or the knowledge I shared reinforced what you already knew. If you are considering abstinence, you will no longer swap stories about sexual escapades with your co-workers. You may lose Bernard Bye-Bye. By no means, is it easy or crowded on this road of righteousness. You may walk alone many, many times. But you are not alone. Know that God sees you.

In your righteous walk, there will be those who mock you as they discover that your walk with God is real. They will accuse you of lying, if you chose to abstain; they will bring up your past; they will assure you that you will never find a suitable mate – which is certainly not true.

Then there will be you – doubting and wondering if maybe they are right. Is this Book we rely on so much for life and liberty outdated? Has it set the bar too high? Is it realistic for someone who has lived a certain way all of their life to be able to just stop, and turn another way, even if it is to God? Sometimes we underestimate our own power. Not only do we have power to impact others, but we have power that makes an impact within our own being.

Gideon was living during a time of disobedience in Israel. Because of their disobedience the LORD allowed the Midianites to have power over His people for seven years. The Midianites would take all of the crops, the sheep and the oxen and leave Israel with no sustenance. The Bible says because of the Midianites, Israel was very low. Can you relate? Sometimes the enemy can invade our space, sometimes because of our own disobedience, and devour everything we have, leaving us with no sustenance.

Israel, like we often do, cried out to the LORD and an angel of the LORD was sent to Gideon as he was beating out wheat to hide in a winepress so that the enemy would not find it. At that point, he seemed as a coward but the angel of the LORD called out to him "O mighty man of valor." God knows what He has placed in us even though we do not always act accordingly.

The angel of the LORD called on him to save Israel, but Gideon informed him that he was weak and the least in his father's house. Can you relate? But the LORD assured him that He was with Him, as He does us. The rest of the story shows us how God prepared Gideon for war *His* way – by taking a little of nothing and doing a whole lot with it.

So shall it be with you. You may only have a little – a less than perfect past, some shattered dreams, some broken promises – but you have some faith and when you place it in God's hand, He will work a miracle and you will be victorious. Do not be afraid, my sister. I have been jotting my thoughts down for you about 3 weeks now. You are in a season of singleness today; chances are the season will change; but in the meantime, get your mind right. How you fare in your singleness is all up to you.

Red Flag: Have confidence in yourself and even more confidence in God. Starting today, focus on the good that God has in store for you and then act accordingly. Don't set yourself up for a life of regrets – of what you could have done or what you should have done when you had the chance. It's all up to you.

Day 28: Know That You Should Yearn for Something More

You should choose life eternally.

This day I call the heavens and the earth as witnesses against
you that I have set before you life and death, blessings and
curses. Now choose life, so that you and your children may live.
—Deuteronomy 30:19 NIV

"You must live in the present, launch yourself on every
wave, find your eternity in each moment. Fools stand
on their island of opportunities and look toward another land;
there is no other life but this." – Henry David Thoreau

Thoreau seems to have captured a common thread sewn
within our western culture. Everywhere we turn our minds
have been inundated by messages that encourage us to live life
to the fullest as if each moment were our last.

As I sat at my cousin's funeral a few years ago, those who
shared found memories of him talked about how he did just
that – lived life to the fullest as if each moment were his last. For
the first time those words, that concept – living each moment as
if it were your last because there is no other life but this – sent
chills through my soul. It almost took my breath away and I
grieved for him even more.

A life filled with "tomorrow's not promised," "take what you
want," "no holds barred" and "whatever makes you feel good"
seems to have given him many, many temporary pleasures, but
no long lived joy – only a tragic death at 40. I want you to know
that the only way to truly live is to live righteously.

Who wants to tip-toe through life, carefully watching,
looking over one's shoulder, anxious about every foot-loose
and fancy-free moment? Not me and probably not you. But

when I consider the results of my actions driven by what I felt, I grieve that, too. For years my decisions, some good and some bad, were made in the heat of what I immediately felt and what I immediately saw. I realized that my feelings were temporary, and my views were obstructed at best.

Hindsight, I can clearly see that the two were so intertwined – what I felt and what I saw – that they seemed as if they were one. Sometimes they came in one sequence – I saw a situation and I felt a certain way about it. Sometimes they came in the other. I felt a certain way about a situation and then I began to see things in that situation that probably were not there. Either way, I responded, either impulsively or selfishly.

Here's an example – I *saw* something I wanted and it excited me so I went for it, without considering the cost (financial, emotional, psychological, spiritual or otherwise). Impulsive.

Here's the flip side of that – I *wanted* something so badly. I saw something that looked close enough to it, so I went for it, convincing myself one of two things – that it was exactly what I wanted or that it was the closest I'd come to it. I didn't consider the cost (or perhaps I did) but my desire far outweighed the cost – at first. Selfish.

I was just doing what Thoreau said – living in the present, launching myself on every wave, finding my eternity in each moment. The problem was, and still is, my eternity was not in any of those moments. Though it looked eternal and felt eternal – it was not.

It took many years before I learned about the effects of impulse. It took many tears before I learned about the results of selfishness – not desiring what you want at any and all cost to others but desiring what your flesh wants above all cost to your spirit or even the Kingdom agenda. So, my dear sister, allow me to spare you some unwanted trouble and undeserved heartache by putting this question on the table: Even when it looks right and it feels right, *is it right*?

How long will we weave in and out of negative outcomes from this decision and that decision on impulse and out of selfishness? Will we ever want anything more than temporary gratification? One sure sign of maturity is being able to say "no" to yourself. Though it may cause discomfort, inconvenience, unhappiness and sometimes embarrassment, you have to want more than everything that is handed to you on a silver platter because contrary to what Thoreau says, there is another life other than "this". There is the after-life, but there is also the "after-this" which is the next circumstance, the next relationship or the next day.

Red Flag: We're coming to the end of our time together. I hope that you will be wise about what you choose to see and hear in all of life's presentations. Today begin to consider righteousness, not only for the "after life," but for the "after this." What you choose to do today will show up again on tomorrow.

Day 29: Know You Will be Okay—Either Way

If you're wondering "But what if I never marry?" you should know you will be fine, too.

If we are thrown into the blazing furnace, the God we serve is able to deliver us from it, and he will deliver us[a] from Your Majesty's hand. [18]But even if he does not, we want you to know, Your Majesty, that we will not serve your gods or worship the image of gold you have set up."
—Daniel 3:17-18 (NIV)

What a place to be! In God there is a place where you are no longer concerned with the question if God will do what He said He will do or even when He will do it. You are in the place where you are resting in the fact that He is *able* to do it. It is the place in God that you trust Him and His plans for you, even if they don't line up with your own desires. If He chooses not to answer your prayers, will it make Him any less God? Any less good? Will you love Him less?

It can be irresponsible of people of faith to act as if they know God's will. People promise us that God will answer our prayers out of their personal desire to see us happy. In my own experience people (those who said they were operating either in the gift of prophecy or in the office of prophet) have approached me with 'words of God' that I received as conformation. Sometimes their words came to fruition; sometimes they did not. While I won't speak too much to this idea because of its sensitivity, I will advise that we don't hang our hopes on the words of others. It's in our nature to look for clues and signs to have some sort of idea when and if God is going to answer our prayers. But we cannot be so consumed with not knowing; this can hi-jack our plans for the present and burden our thoughts for the future. We must learn to trust God for the day He has us in. If we do not, we will miss it all together and long for it once it has passed.

Each and every day is filled with so many wonders of God. He is working in and around us. The prophet Jeremiah proclaimed His mercies are new every morning (Lamentations 3:23). So rich is His love for us and it is proven every day; yes, both good and bad days. I submit that when we look hindsight, we recognize that even our bad days turned out for our good.

When we trust God, it is not just for the moments that we see; it is also for the moments that we don't – moments in the future. Jesus admonishes us not to be concerned about our needs. He tells us that God will supply *all of them* just as He does for the birds of the air. "Are you not more valuable than they?" (Matthew 6: 26 NIV). How many times have you tossed and turned all night worried about an impending doom happening on the next day and when you actually got to the next day… nothing happened…or something happened but it wasn't what you thought it would be? Fear hi-jacked your good night's sleep. Worry held your peace hostage for the night and all for naught.

Our Father is looking out for us and He has a proven track record of doing so. Whatever it is you fear that you will lack if you find yourself single for the rest of your life, know there is no lack in God. Remember the first verse in Psalm 23…*you shall not want*. He keeps us content in whatever situation we find ourselves. He has the power to do so. He can grant contentment when we are well, when we are sick; when we have money and when we don't; when we are married and when we are not.

Marriage will bring many things to your life; but what it will *not bring* is complete happiness. You have good and bad days when you are single; you will have good and bad days when you are married. You can be broke when you are single; you can be broke once you get married (but now there are twice as many expenses). You can have issues with *your* family; you can have issues with your family *and his, too.* The same God you need in your singleness today is the same God you will need in your marriage tomorrow and for all of life's challenges. So why burden your future with doubt and fear when He is already in your future, working out whatever life brings *or does not*?

Red Flag: Trust in the LORD whether He delivers you *or not*; trust His will even if it's not your want. I pray that you will release your future today and allow it to flourish in your tomorrow.

Day 30: Zoom in on Your Future, I Know You Want To

*And finally, I want you to know that any pain or emptiness you
have so far survived has both a reason and a reward. Look for it!
Even if it's not blatantly in your face, it will be there!*

For I know the thoughts I think toward you, saith the LORD,
thoughts of peace, and not of evil, to give you
an expected end.
—Jeremiah 29:11 KJV

There will be peace where this is obedience to God. There will
be self-control. There will be patience. There will be trust.
There will be wholeness. There will be growth! There will be
liveliness. There will be hope. There will be adventure. There
will be romance, yes, romance! There will be true intimacy and
there will be real love. Most of all, there will be righteousness in
a place where there is obedience to God.

I can clearly see it there so I'm zooming in on your future
and you should, too! No matter how hard it gets, no matter how
lonely it gets, no matter how frustrated you get, don't look to
the left or to the right or down or around. Focus and you will
see God clearly.

Let's end with something familiar.

Jeremiah was known as the weeping prophet. He lamented
over the state of his beloved Israel. It seemed to have been his
life's work warning them of destruction and captivity. But the
LORD also used Jeremiah as a beacon of hope once Judah had
been taken captive.

During this time there were many false prophets saying that
their stay in Babylon would be short-lived. To the contrary, the
word of the LORD had already been spoken by His true prophet,

Jeremiah. So he writes a letter to those in exile confirming that their time in Babylon would be no shorter than the 70 years God had allotted. He encourages them to go ahead and settle in, as they would in their own land, even advising them to pray for the welfare of Babylon. Their own welfare was now connected to Babylon. He warns them not to get caught up in false hope which the false prophets brought, but rest assured that God would return them to their land *at the appointed time*.

Though they were in bondage and longed for that which they loved, God had not left them. This season in their lives was a part of God's plan and His plan had not changed. He still had a hope and a future for them (Jeremiah 29:11). Jeremiah, in essence, writes to his people to trust the process. Though at times they may have felt alone and deserted, God had not forgotten them. The same is for you. Be at peace and rest in Him. He is still a very present God who has promised never to leave you nor forsake you. He is preparing a beautiful future for you.

Red Flag: I wrote this exhortation so that you will never feel uncovered or unkept in your singleness though it is so easy to do so. It is my prayer that today you will begin to feel God's presence and know that He is there. Though you may be in an uncomfortable place, zoom in on the expected end. Know for sure it is there!

About the Author

Penny Suber Staten is not a name that you would hear across the globe. She is not a prominent inspirational speaker, nor is she a New York Times Best Seller; but Penny Suber Staten is simply a woman who genuinely loves God, has a hope in His Word, a passion for His daughters and a desire to see them live free from pain, from distraction and repercussions.

A prolific writer, she is a poet, a workshop clinician and a field representative for Urban Ministries Inc, the largest independent African American owned and operated Christian media company. Penny is also the author of *Temple Renovation 52, A Practical Guide to Maintaining Abstinence in the 21st Century*, and *Red Flags: What Single Women Should Know*.

She is a graduate of the College of Biblical Studies with a Bachelor of Science degree in Women's Ministry. She is currently matriculating at Faith International Seminary, and will soon earn her Master's degree in Christian Education.

Penny is married to Pastor Dr. Steven C. Staten, and together they enjoy four sons and two daughters, in addition to a son- and daughter-in-love.

Follow Penny on Instagram at 52.ministries.

www.ingramcontent.com/pod-product-compliance
Lightning Source LLC
Chambersburg PA
CBHW071947100426
42736CB00042B/2301